BUTTERFLY BEGINNINGS

Arethea Martin Green

Butterfly Beginnings

From the Shadows of the Steeple...

By Arethea Martin Green

"...be ye steadfast, unmovable, always abounding in the work of the Lord..."

1 Corinthians 15:58

COPYRIGHT

Printed in the United States of America

First Printing, 2015

ISBN-13: 978-1-942022-07-7

the **B**utterfly Typeface

Iris M Williams - Owner

PO Box 56193
Little Rock, AR 72215

THE BUTTERFLY TYPEFACE PUBLISHING

THE GOAL of The Butterfly Typeface Publishing 'spread' a message of inspiration, imagination and intrigue. We strive to 'transform' the ordinary into something EXTRA-ordinary!

Whether you hire us to edit, ghostwrite, publish (books & magazines) or design a website, you are guaranteed exemplary customer service, fairness and quality.

Our vision, under God's leadership, is to serve and assist in the healing of the heart, mind and soul of *all* people we encounter with integrity, intentional influence and positive purpose.

"We make good GREAT!"

"Not that we are sufficient of ourselves
to think anything as of ourselves;
but our sufficiency is of God"

II Corinthians 3:5

DEDICATION

Therefore this book is dedicated to the Lord God my Saviour, the one that created me, saved me, and strengthens me. To Him and Him alone do I owe "All" for He has done great things for me and I am forever grateful.

The Arethea Martin Green Butterfly!

BUTTERFLIES

Butterflies are different and quite unique
For when they start out, they are as ugly as can be

They hide in a cocoon many days and nights
Then when they come out, what a beautiful sight

Butterflies are in one way similar to you and me
We all choose our way of life,
but not the color that we will be

The next glance of a butterfly, please do think of others
We all know the same 'Creator',
yet we are all different colors

All butterflies are not identical, there are no two the same
God made them on purpose, Adam gave them their name

No matter if you are average, purple, black or white
Just like the butterfly, God made you just right

-Arethea Martin Green

TABLE OF CONTENTS

FOREWORD

"When you learn, teach, when you get, give."

-Maya Angelou

MAYA ANGELOU was simple, yet oh so complex. She did not look like what she had been through – no, her beauty was timeless, humble and classic. She loved foundationally and when I heard her tell someone she loved them, I instinctively knew she meant it.

While Maya was a sweet and gentle soul, she was also a force to be reckoned with. She knew she was phenomenal and she refused to allow her song to remain caged.

Maya STOODOUT – she was a grand lady with a grand assignment.

I believe her assignment was to give which is why she was blessed with so much …

Why am I speaking about Maya Angelou at this time, you ask? Well because my Godfriend Arethea epitomizes Maya Angelou.

She isn't as tall as Maya was, but she has a giant presence just the same. Like Maya, Arethea speaks with purpose and intention. She loves God and gains joy simply from knowing that Jesus died for you and me.

Like Maya, Aretha's words weave wonder and creates in you a stirring and a knowing. As a great writer should, she inspires me to be a better writer, friend and Christian.

Arethea STANDS OUT in a crowd. Not because she desires to, but because God's light shines so brightly inside of her.

She is a *grand lady* with a *grand assignment.* I believe her assignment is to *give* which is why she has been blessed with so much … and greater is yet to come!

I thank God for sending you my way. I thank you for trusting me with your words. I thank you for your friendship and love. I love you dearly.

May God bless you so abundantly that you have not room enough for which to receive!

-Iris M Williams
Author/Publisher

ACKNOWLEDGMENTS

GOD'S BLESSINGS and favor upon the owner and founder of *The Butterfly Typeface Publishing*, Iris M Williams. There are not enough words to convey how all of this came together. The best way that I can explain or describe it is simply by saying … But God!

To my daughter Anyonita Jenea Green Boyles, the only girl that God gave us – Thank you for always saying, "Mama you have to write something!" She is my inspiration and has been there since day one – years ago!

-Arethea Martin Green

THE BEGINNING

MY DESIRE and prayer is that everyone that reads this devotional would see not the author but the God of the author. That you would find yourself somewhere within this book that might cause you to be closer drawn to Him.

It is also my desire that this devotional will become a year-to-year journal that you will highlight, make notes and list prayer requests.

If you are led to do so, go back and measure your growth and answered prayers. Take Him at His word. What a great God we serve.

God bless your life!

Grace & Mercy

ATTITUDE

The Love of Luke

IN LUKE chapter 15, we read a familiar passage of scripture. The chapter contains a parable about The Lost Sheep. A parable is an earthly story with a heavenly meaning. As soon as the parable began, Jesus allows us to see that not all people will rejoice with us in life's events **(verses 1-2)** He began to share the three illustrations of rejoicing:

Illustration #1: **Verse 4**. *"What man having a hundred sheep when he lose one of them does not leave the ninety-nine to go and find the one and when he hath found him layeth it on his shoulders rejoicing, and when he cometh home saith unto his friends and neighbors rejoice with me."*

Illustration #2: **Verse 8**. *"Either what woman having ten pieces of silver if she lose one piece doth not light a candle, and sweep the house, and seek diligently till she find it? And when she hath found it, she calleth her friends and her neighbors together, saying, Rejoice with me, for I have found the piece which I had lost."* Jesus reminds us that the angels in heaven rejoiceth over one that repenteth (**Verse 10**).

Illustration #3: **Verses 11-32**. *"And he said, A certain man had 2two sons ...."*

As we go back and rethink these verses, there is so much to gather from *Luke chapter 15*. In **verses 12-16** the youngest son asks his father to give him the portion of goods that falleth upon him. As parents we know when things will not turn out well for our children, just as the Father knows for us. We, just like The Father, allow their will to be done. We realize that we must allow them to see things for themselves.

The son went out, not many days later and wasted all that he had in riotous living, as most rebellious children do. After he had spent all, his only choice was to feed the pigs and eat what they ate.

Verse 17 He comes to himself and realize that his father's servants had better living conditions and food than he had.

Verse 18-19 He decides to go back home and repent of sinning to both his earthly father and heavenly Father.

Verse 20 He rose up and started home, but before he could get there his father saw him had compassion hugged his neck, and kissed him. Just as our Heavenly Father knows when we will return back to Him after the world has beat us down! He welcomes us home over and over again because He loves us!

Verse 21 The son admits his sin to his father and confesses that he also sinned against God.

Verse 22 The father sends the servant for a robe, ring and to make a fatted calf to celebrate the coming of his son back home.

What a blessing to know that our Father, does the exact same for us, He said in Hebrews that He would never leave us nor forsake us!!! His father made mention that his son that was once spiritually dead was now alive.

During this merry time in their lives there was another family member that was going to put a damper on things!!! Even in our lives when there is a merry time, there might be someone that will not be happy for our blessing.

Verse 25 As the oldest son is leaving the fields he hears music and dancing as he approaches the house. He asks a servant, in our terminology. "What is going on?" When the servant tells him he is Hot!!!

Verse 28 He is so angry that he does not want to go into the house. His father comes out and begs him to come in.

Verse 29 He is so angry that that he disrespects his father. Read verse 29, He is basically saying all these years I did right for nothing. "You never gave me a fatted calf to make merry with my friends!"

Verse 30 He is so mad that he does not acknowledge his youngest brother as his brother, he continues to mention him to his father as "your son".

Verse 31-32 His father reminds him that he has him always and that now is the time to rejoice for his brother.

There is so much to learn as Christians from this parable.

1. The oldest son had a "Bad Attitude" he was in the house but not in fellowship with his father. Just as Christians we can be in the house of the Lord, but no be in fellowship with Him, we can be sitting but not serving!
2. Bad attitudes can cause others to leave the house. The oldest brother may have caused the youngest to leave home because of his bad attitude. Christians can also cause other

Christians to leave the Lord's house and never attend church again.

3. A bad attitude can cause us not to rejoice with others, when a Christian Brother or Sister returns back to the Lord.
4. A bad attitude can cause us to disrespect those that have authority over us. The oldest son disrespected his father.
5. The Lord will always send someone to remind us of His goodness toward us. The father reminded his oldest son that he was always with him and that what he had was also the son's. The same applies to us The Father is always with us and all that He has He wants us to receive from Him.
6. We must remember that just as the prodigal son's sins were forgiven, so are ours if we confess our sins to Him. **1John 1:9**

Thank God for His Holy Word that teaches, leads and guides us daily.

QUESTIONS TO PONDER

What incident in your life is relative to Luke Chapter 15?

Was there someone in your life who warned you of the possible outcome?

What lesson did you learn from the experience you listed above?

Have you made the above mistake (Or any other mistake) more than once? If so, why?

How forgiving are you towards someone who repeatedly makes the same mistake towards you?

FAITH

Even When He Is In The House, There Will Be Doubters

"And again he entered into Caperaum after some days; and it was noised that he was in the house. And straightway many gathered together, insomuch that there was no room to receive them, no, not so much as about the door: and he preached the word unto them." **Mark 2:1-2**

WHILE READING my devotions today my mind wondered, "What moves people?" What compels them to serve the Lord with so much joy and faithfulness? What also at the same time causes others to bicker and complain and speak doubt into the minds of other Christians?

Ever notice how within our home, church and family gatherings there is always that group that is happy and excited and ready to do whatever necessary to help? Then there is that one or group that talks everything down, never a positive remark? No matter what is right it's never right in their eyesight.

Reading this passage this morning blessed and encouraged me so much. It reminded me that even

'When He is in The House, There Will Be Doubters.' It took me back to the time that I rededicated my life back to the Lord in 1987 there were so many friends that always doubted that I was sincere. They did all that they could to cast doubt on the very thing that I knew to be true, something that took place in my life yet they tried to cast doubt.

In our homes we can pray all day every day and do our very best to please our families. Both spouses can work full time jobs they may even have and provide the finest things for themselves and children.

That home may be spirit-filled and prayed in and over daily and even when He is in the house, there will still be family members that are doubters.

I would often tell my children when they were young and we would sing Amazing Grace, I would remind them that yes, they sing that song and one day when they are older they would experience that Amazing Grace. It is one thing to sing it, but it is something totally different once you have witnessed it.

Our children, when they are young, tend to doubt our faith and even God's ability to work in and through our lives and family problems, so they become household doubters. As they mature and grow older marry and they have children it is then that they experience the goodness of God on a completely different level.

In the local church the pastor can toil and pray all week long for the message from God for God's people. Many times that message may not come until Thursday, Friday or sometimes not until Sunday morning, because that's just how the Lord works.

Nevertheless, the pastor can preach and the Holy Spirit can be all over the church and in the hearts of God's people, but even then *'When He Is In The House, There Will Be Doubters.'* Doubters are everywhere that we are. In **Mark 2:2-5** when the man that was sick of the palsy friends could not get him in the house to see Jesus they made a way. They cut a hole in the roof to get him there. They lowered him through his sins were forgiven and he was healed. Even though Jesus himself was in the house that day God in the flesh! There were still doubters, and if there were doubters on that day we better believe that we will always have to deal with doubters in our lives.

Jesus dealt with his doubters immediately when he perceived in his spirit Jesus proved to them who he was. Only Jesus can heal and forgive. **Verse 6-8** is a great example of Jesus dealing with them and we must also deal with our doubters when we are confronted. We must help them to cast all doubt away. We must show them that Only Jesus can save, heal and forgive. Many doubt because no one has ever told them that Jesus saves and He cares let it not be said of us that we perceived in our spirit that they doubted yet we dealt not with them.

QUESTIONS TO PONDER

What moves or compels you to serve God? Why do you think some doubt God's existence?

_____

_____

Do you have those that doubt your sincerity? Have they tried to undermine you? Elaborate.

_____

_____

Have you witnessed God's Amazing Grace? Elaborate.

_____

_____

Why is it important to confront the doubters?

_____

_____

What are some ways you can confront the doubters?

_____

_____

MANIPULATION

Control Freaks & Micromanagers
(Even In the Church)

FOR MANY years I have wondered what makes people feel the need to maintain control at all times. To always desire the need to be in full control of everything and all things. While reading a book one day on personality traits, this type personality stayed on my mind. Choleric, this best describes to me the control freak personality. This type person or group of people are often in the home, work place, neighborhood and sad to say the church. The choleric trait personality is described as one that is powerful, tireless worker, makes quick decisions and goal oriented. Their weaknesses are usually always right, impatient, lacks compassion, and must always be in control.

This choleric type personality is a person that you may have to deal with often depending on who the person is. Whether in the home, work, or church there may be problems when this person comes around. If they are a Christian it is even worse because this Christian sister or brother may be someone that you minister with week in and out. It is most times that faithful or annoying one. This a Christian sister or brother that may have never been confronted by anyone, because who would dare come up against them?

They are that Christian that has faithfully served in many areas that have also occasionally spoken out for a worthy cause.

This is that Christian that also deserves to be loved and respected, but again never approached. Yet this is that Christian that needs to be counseled in love with the Bible close at hand. This Christian must be shown themselves in the Bible. **Ecc.1:9** reads, *"The thing that have been, it is not which shall be done; and there is no new thing under the sun."* In other words if it happened in God's time, it will happen in ours.

John dealt with the very same thing in **3John**, John was commending Gaius an elder that he loved. He was commending him on his faithfulness, and the way that others were faithfully serving and walking in the truth. John was excited for them he was encouraging them! (I encourage you to go back and read this wonderful passage) In verse **9 John** said, *"I wrote unto the church but Diotrephes, who loveth to have the preeminence among them receiveth us not."* As we continue to read John says, (Paraphrased) I will remember his deeds which he does causing confusion and running his mouth.

John 11 reads, *"Beloved, follow not that which is evil, but that which is good. He that doeth good is of God: but he that doeth evil hath not seen God."*

In other words John is saying have no dealing with Christians that must always be in control after you have tried to biblically warn then and counseled with them.

John said the he had more to write but he would just wait until he sees them. **Verse 13, Verse 14** I think John was just like us when we deal with people that profess to be Christians. He had just had enough and was done for the day. His spirit may have been dampened from dealing with Diotresphes.

The Christian that is a control freak, micromanager, or choleric, whatever we choose to describe them as, can kill any church or ministry. At some point they are to be pulled aside if it is out of control. Usually there are one or more in every church. The Lord gave me this devotion to write last year when I was reading the passage. I immediately thought of this title Control Freaks. God bless the church and it's ministry that does not have Christians with this type personality, and God bless the ministry that does, I have found that a few good verses to share along with many others may be.

"Great peace have they which love thy law: and nothing shall offend them." **Psalms 119:165**

"Am I therefore become your enemy, because I tell you the truth?" **Galatians 4:16**

QUESTIONS TO PONDER

Are you a control freak? If so, how do you know? If not, do you know one? Describe traits.

_____

_____

Why do you think control freaks exist in the church?

_____

_____

How would you counsel a control freak?

_____

_____

What would you do if you counsel was not received? Would you try again?

_____

_____

How would you distance yourself from a control freak that you MUST encounter daily?

_____

_____

Growth

LOVE

IT'S NOT JUST A WEDGE

SEVERAL YEARS ago a preacher friend of mine preached, what I would describe as a unique message about a wedge. His illustration was liken to that of cutting down a tall tree. He said "When one is cutting down a tall tree one good way is to make a wedge, then proceed to make deeper and deeper on the opposite side of where you wanted the tree to fall," After constantly cutting into the tree you should apply the rope around it and the tree does eventually fall."

Well, it then appeared to me that this same truth could be applied to marital or friend relationships that might be on the verge of going bad, at the beginning we form a wedge. We forget as Christians that **Psalm 34:13** reads, *"Keep thy tongue from evil and thy lips from speaking guile."* We began to cut and devour, we are inconsiderate of each other's feelings. We become unloving and after a while we may even began to major on the negatives, we nick pick personality traits. We allow room for pride to set in, everything has to be our way right away.

At this point self-righteousness can very easily command control, we are far from remembering the power and importance of prayer. **Proverbs 17:17** reads, *"A friend loveth at all times, and a brother is born for adversity."* We forget that this person is someone we started out loving. If we are not careful the situation (or the wedge) can become wider and wider. **Proverbs 15:1** is also far from our thoughts, *"A soft answer turneth away wrath; but grievous words stir up anger."* We began to slowly fall out of grace and love, because the devil is now raising his head and stirring us to enlarge our wedge.

Friendships and marriages both share the common bond of 'Love'. No relationship can ever be formed without love, love is vast and is many things. Love is described by all with a different terminology. No one can truly say what love is outside of what God has ordained in **1 Corinthians 13**. We all would have to agree that what love is to one may not be the same to another. The greatness of true Christian love, be it through marriage or friendship, has to be God ordained because He is the personification of love. Even just mentioning it now, I tend to get off course because God's love is powerful.

Getting back to that wedge, if we as Christians could fully grasp the depth of a wedge: and the hurt that it may cause, we would all be closer drawn to Him.

Words do hurt and once they proceed out of our mouths we cannot gather them up again. The final to this devotion is that once that wedge is driven and cut into and it becomes so wide, then we launch the rope of "It's all your fault" around it that particular tree or relationship will most definitely come crashing down!

Psalm 34:13-14 reads, *"Keep thy tongue from evil, and thy lips from speaking guile. Depart from evil, and do good; seek peace and pursue it."*

As a Christians I know how hard it is to do what is required both in a marital and relationship with friends. The comfort I have is remembering that we became friends because I loved them. We can all learn from the Master Teacher Jesus, He says in **John 3:16** *"For God so loved the world that He gave His only begotten Son, that whosoever believeth in Him shall not perish, but have everlasting life."*

We all need to choose to love unconditionally and His way. I am most grateful that He gave me this devotion to write, for I have much need of His teachings in my life.

QUESTIONS TO PONDER

Is there a wedge in your relationship (marital, family or friend)? How has it manifested?

_____

_____

What impact is this wedge having on your relationship?

_____

_____

Are wedges 'fixable'? If so, what can you do to fix the wedge?

_____

_____

What does love mean to you? Do you and your spouse/family/friend have same definition?

_____

_____

How can remembering 'why' you love someone benefit the relationship during rough times?

_____

_____

PAIN

New Things Can Be Birthed Through Pain

IN AUGUST of 2012 and again in August of 2013, my husband was hospitalized with what they found to be infection of the blood. The mystery is that they had no name for it, nor could they find a cause. Both times it was life threatening. God, with His hand of mercy saw fit to allow my husband to live.

This life changing event came as a huge surprise to us, we were not expecting him to be sick and we definitely were not expecting him to be in the hospital for five months. During this time we remembered that as things occur to us they were never a surprise to the Lord. There are no surprises to Him. Neither are there surprises in Him. He was already there before us and we could feel His presence and the prayers of His people surrounding us.

It is so amazing that we can know of someone that may be battling cancer or some other type of sickness and we can see them spending these their last few days upon this earth; yet we are all surprised when they take that final breath. The loss of this person still bears much pain within our hearts we also rejoice because we know that if they were born again they are with the Lord.

Struggle is normal in the Christian life. We are not to ever feel because we are Christians that we are exempt from struggles, heartache or pain.

"For if we be dead with him, we shall also live with him: if we suffer, we shall also reign with him: if we deny him, he also will deny us." **II Timothy 2:11, 12**

Out of both pain and struggles new things can be birthed. Some of the most profound spiritual things happen in our lives during these times. If we would mentally place Jesus in the midst of our pain, struggles, trials etc., we would have great comfort. Why would I say 'mentally' place Him? Because we know that physically He is already there, we just cannot see Him with our human eyes.

When He is in that key place, there He can begin to minister to our every need. He will walk us through the present situation and show us great and mighty things if we allow Him to do so. He will lead us to scriptures and people to pray with us and assure us of His power over our lives. He will provide rest beyond measure all because we are resting in Him.

When all of this is over we will have restored strength and renewed faith.

"Thou will keep him in perfect peace, whose mind is stayed on thee: because he trusteth in thee." **Isaiah 26:3**

When things are going on in our lives, we tend to lose focus especially if we are the type to desire to gain control. This is the perfect time to stop and allow the God that created us, that knows what is best, to have His way.

Within the illness of my husband, great things were birthed in my life. First, I was drawn closer to Him in a way that I had never before. Secondly, I realized that He was the 'only' one that could allow my husband to continue to live. No one in this world could do that for us. Thirdly, as my husband's spouse I had to pray for both of us because at this state he could not pray for himself. Fourth, God at this time had my 'undivided attention'. Nothing else in life mattered more to me. Lastly, because of my walk with Him, I knew that I could trust Him to do what was best and that which would be His will.

Jesus is my friend. He is not someone that I *only* call on when I am in need. I love Him and I pray and spend time with Him daily. I knew that if He decided to call my husband home, that He would continue to provide for me and meet my every need and desire.

I am by no means a 'super saint' because that title does 'NO MAN' hold, but I am telling you that He knows me in a way that I have grown closer to Him over the years. I have trusted Him far more times than before now and He has never failed me yet – and He never will.

I am forever grateful to Him and the faithful family and friends that were there to pray us through and that remain in our lives today. I thank Him for the great things that were birthed through this storm in our lives. Among other scriptures the following was a great comfort to me.

"Now unto him that is able to keep you from falling, and to present you faultless before the presence of his glory with exceeding joy. To the only wise God our Saviour, be glory and majesty, dominion and power, both now and ever. Amen." **Jude 24, 25**

My friend, great things can be birthed through pain if we allow Jesus to have full control. When we are in the middle of the crisis, listen to His still small voice.

QUESTIONS TO PONDER

What was spiritually birthed through your last trial?

_____

_____

What scripture did you read the most to bring your comfort?

_____

_____

What key person/people did the Lord use to encourage you during this time?

_____

_____

Have you used this event to share with other believers or non-believers?

_____

_____

What was your initial response to this trial? Where were you when it took place?

_____

_____

CHANGE

Accepting the Fact
That People Do Change

AS THE PASTOR gave the scripture reference for his message, **Acts 9**, something caught my attention. Later that afternoon I went back and read it and the Lord gave me this devotion. The entire passage of **Acts 9** had never appeared to me as it had that day.

Saul knew that he had changed for he had been struck blind on the road to Damascus, but as he came to Jerusalem to join the disciples they did not accept him. Saul had experienced something in his life, but because of the way he had persecuted Christians in the past they did not believe that he had been converted. There is nothing new under the sun. **Ecclesiastes 1:9** reads, *"The thing that hath been, it is that which shall be; and that which is done is that which shall be done: and there is no new thing under the sun."*

As I read **Acts 9** that day, I immediately became convicted. I was as guilty as the disciples were that day. I had not always accepted others that were changed. I did not embrace them at the first - I doubted their conversion. I was not a Barnabas, he embraced Saul and led him along the way. I am grateful that the Lord allowed me to reread **Acts 9** because it allowed me to see that I responded just as the disciples had. After all, salvation is an individual spiritual experience, that over flows to the outside, as we share our conversion our new walk in Him can give Him the glory and point others to His saving grace and power.

God left us complete details with many examples of things that would take place in our lives. Whatever it is, He covered it within the bible. It is not a coincidence that either we or someone that we know has experienced the very thing that happened to Saul - after his conversion God changed his name to Paul. It is not a new thing when people become SAVED, if they lived a life that would seem hard to believe that they could change, they are treated as Saul was.

It is normal but not new to respond this way when we encounter the new birth of a family member or friend or ourselves. Why is it so hard to accept them? One reason would be, because they may have lived such a rebellious life and we just could not envision them ever coming to know the Lord.

Therefore we respond as the disciples did, at the first only Barnabas embraced him. Sometimes it might be just one person for us as well at first. Just as Paul did, we too have to prove our conversion to some people. That is okay - continue to read about the life of Paul if you haven't. Paul is one of my favorite disciples. I love to read his writings. In doing so you can truly see that the Lord uses those that are willing to repent and believe on Him. He would not have given us His word if it wasn't going to transform our lives. No one is perfect only the Lord **Romans 3:23**. Jesus Christ makes that clear to us, there is not day that we will ever measure up to God. Paul's life was changed because he met the Master. No one that has ever come to Him and accepted His free gift and believed on Him has walked away the same. He told the woman at the well if she drank the water from the well she would have just quenched her thirst but if she drank of His water she would NEVER thirst again! **John 4:7**

All Christians know that to be true, for He was given us the drink of eternal life with Him, because we believed on Him and the Death, Burial, and Resurrection of Him. We are not trusting in ourselves but Him to take us to heaven when we die. **Romans 10:9** reads, *"That if thou shalt confess with thou mouth the Lord Jesus, and shalt believe in thine heart that God hath raised him from the dead, thou shalt be saved."*

Paul believed yet he was not accepted at first, yet he continued on with his walk in the Lord. He knew in his heart what the Lord had done for him. When we meet someone that we knew would have been a hard case to win to Jesus how will we respond? Think about Saul/Paul give them a chance to walk out their salvation; don't be too quick to judge. Embrace them and encourage them, even if you have doubt, just keep it to yourself and encourage them for they will need it, just as we all do and always will.

QUESTIONS TO PONDER

What was it like for you when you accepted Christ as your Saviour?

_____

_____

Did you change? Were others accepting? Why or why not?

_____

_____

How might a person feel who has changed but their change is not accepted?

_____

_____

Have you ever witnessed a Saul/Paul conversion in someone else? If so how did you respond?

_____

_____

If you responded like the disciples would you be willing to go back and share this devotion with that person?

_____

_____

Obedience

PRAYER

What Is Going On In Your Town?

"Woe To the bloody city! It is full of lies and robbery; the prey departeth not;" **Nahum 3:1**

THIS COULD be the headline for any state, city or town, across America or around the world. I have no desire to listen to the news most mornings and evenings. It is hard to believe that all around the world there is devastating news continually.

Events that we probably would have thought we'd never hear of are now taking place on a daily basis. Years ago the news and newspaper were shared as a family and it was read for good things and not bad. It was a joy to do the crossword puzzles, comics and for some the horoscopes.

If you were a woman you looked for coupons to clip to save money at the local stores. If you were a man you enjoyed gazing at that new truck that you so desperately desired. Well, some of these things still exist; women are far better now at couponing and men still truck watch. However, there are fewer newspapers delivered to the home. As time changes so does things, but for some reason we all hope that crime and robbery and the taking of one's lives would not be a thing that would get worse instead of better.

Unfortunately, that is where we are and chances are that all these things will continue to increase and not decrease. The Lord God destroyed the earth for the sin of man. **Genesis 6:13** reads, *"And God said unto Noah, the end of all flesh is come before me, for the earth is filled with violence through them; and, behold, I will destroy them with the earth."* Only Noah, his wife, three son and their wives were save alive along with the animals. After the flood God made a promise that He would never curse the land again from the sin of man. God said even though the imagination of man was evil from his youth. **Genesis 8:21**

Ninevah was also a city just as we have today, even after Jonah finally went there to preach repentance to them, after a while they went right back to their old ways. God said in **Nahum 2:8** *"But Ninevah is of old like a pool of water:"* God did destroy their city just as He did Sodom and Gomorrah for their wickedness. Lot begged God not to destroy them if he found 50, 40, 30, 20, 10… righteous people there, God granted him that desire but there were now to be found. God promised that He would not destroy the earth again because of sin, so what are we to do as Christians because of all that is going on? What can we do to help our city?

- ❖ We can continue to pray! **1Thessalonians 5:17** reads, *"Pray without ceasing."*
- ❖ Pray for religious leaders and those that serve under them. **Thessolonians 3:1-2** reads, *"Finally, Brethren, pray for us, that the word of the Lord may have free course, and be glorified, even as it is with you, And that we may be delivered from unreasonable and wicked men: for all men have not faith."*
- ❖ Pray for more Christian workers. **Matthew 9:37** reads, *"Then saith he unto his disciples, The harvest truly is plenteous, but the labourers are few."*
- ❖ Pray for and with your family and friends.
- ❖ Pray, participate, and support community events that reach out to the saved and the unsaved.
- ❖ Do not give up on your city, pray for its local leaders, and send them a card of encouragement.
- ❖ Remember that God is the God of all cities, He never sleeps. **Psalm 121:4** Behold, he that keepeth Israel shall neither slumber nor sleep.

QUESTIONS TO PONDER

What incident in your town (or the world) do you feel needs prayer?

Why do you think prayer is what is needed in this situation?

Has there been past situations where you've seen prayer change a town?

Do you believe that prayer can work on such a large scale? Why or why not?

Can you list examples of other things that are going on in your town or around the world that requires prayer?

ENDURANCE

Short Cuts

THE VERY NIGHT that I am excited that I get to go to bed the Lord lays this devotion on my heart. One afternoon, I had just pulled into the driveway and I see two of my neighbor's dogs running towards our house. I immediately thought that this was the reason that the Lord had lead me to back in, so that these dogs would not catch me off guard. In a split second all of a sudden the two dogs jetted across and ran behind another neighbor's house. I thought that they may have caught a glimpse of another dog and was headed that way. That was not the case these dogs were using what appeared to be human minds and were taking a 'Short Cut' back to their master's house. It was quite humorous that they were doing such a thing. Even as dogs they realized that going a different route would afford them a faster time of getting back home.

As Christians we often take 'Short Cuts' not realizing, or not knowing that the longest way unlike the dogs is actually the best way for us. We live in a world that dictates that faster is better, that does not apply to the Christian walk. Being and becoming a Christian requires a patience. **Isaiah 30:21** reads, *"And thine ears shall hear a word behind thee saying, This is the way, walk ye in it........"* No as Christians we will not hear this audibly because God no longer speaks in this form today, but through His word therefore spiritually we hear Him as we spend time in His word and through prayer.

When we are tempted to go another direction other than that which the Lord has shown us, then we unlike my neighbor's dogs will not end up at our Master's house. **Micah 6:8** reads, *"He hath shewed thee, O man, what is good; and what doth the Lord require of thee, but to do justly, and to love mercy, and walk humbly with thy God?"* There is no Christian without excuse because we have the bible as our road map and the Lord has given us others to encourage us along the way; not just to be encouraged but to also encourage others. We are not perfect by any means. **Proverbs 24:16** tells us that, *"For a just man falleth seven times, and riseth up again: but the wicked shall fall into mischief."*

It is not if, but when we fall short of the desires of the Lord for our lives, we need to all be spiritually prepared as to how to properly respond. We must also remember and realize that **1John 1:9** applies to every believer, *"If we confess our sins, he is faithful and just to forgive us our sins, and cleanse us from all unrighteousness."* We must always know that we are not alone in this Christian walk; the Lord is forever present and He will show us if we come to Him. **Psalm 16:11** reads, *"Thou will shew me the path of life: in his presence is fullness of joy; at thou right hand there are pleasures for evermore."*

'*Short Cuts*' that are not ordained of God is dangerous for Christians. I do not mean backsliding, I mean backsliding and staying backslidden, the Lord has no pleasure in that. **Psalm 23:3** *"... he leadeth me in the path of righteousness for his name sake."* It is all for the sake that we bear His name that He wants what is best for us.

'Short Cuts' will cause me, you and others to become spiritually shipwrecked. In this walk we never quit alone, we sometimes cause others to follow our horrible decisions. Remain encouraged and encourage others that 'Short Cuts' are good *only* if they will lead us back to 'Our Master's House.'

QUESTIONS TO PONDER

Have you taken 'short cuts' in life that you later regretted? If so what happened?

_____

_____

What do you think would have happened if you had taken the long route? What would you have learned?

_____

_____

Have you backslide before? What happened?

_____

_____

How did you recover from backsliding?

_____

_____

What advice do you have to help others who may have backslidden?

_____

_____

MEDITATION

In The Secret Place

"He that dwelleth in the secret place of the most high shall abide under the shadow of the Almighty." **Psalm 91:1**

THE LORD YEARNS to dwell in a secret, special place with us even at our convenience. Where is that secret place for you? Does the Lord have to cause a storm in our lives to get us to that secret place? I have two places in my home that I love to meet with the Lord and share my heart with him. I usually sit or lay and just meditate and tell Him, how much I appreciate His love and goodness towards me. It is the perfect place of spiritual solace.

"I love them that love me; and those that seek me early shall find me." **Psalms 8:17**

Years ago when I read that scripture I felt good because I am an early riser and being with Him early during my devotions was a refreshing time for me. Did God mean that only those that meet with Him early in the morning He loves most? No, of course not, that verse can be thought of in many ways. God delights in early salvation from us because we would have longer to spend with Him in life.

I am pretty sure that is has something to do with accepting Him as our Saviour, as soon as we realize that He came to die for us.

"God is a jealous God..." **Nahum 1:2**

He longs to be with us and to be a part of us on a daily basis. He wants us to pray to Him, not just when we are lonely or need an answered prayer. He longs to be a part of our conversations and our goals in life. He wants to be invited, although He is already there. He desires to have His word hidden in our hearts and spoken of with our lips.

It is always so refreshing to me, to visit my friends' homes and get a sense of His presences, then to see and read things that they display that remind me of Him, His promises I our lives and the way that He has blessed them.

When we would travel as a family we would pray before road trips and before leaving for school each day. That is one thing that I miss the most about our children being adults, the times that we would pray together.

God commended Moses because He knew that he would tell his children of Him. We as Christians should be doing the same with our children/grandchildren if we have any. It is very important that we leave a biblical heritage of Him to them of first salvation, then baptism, prayer and extended prayer towards others.

The blessing of the secret place is God will meet us there. He will accept our invitation to come. He will show up as often as He is invited. As for me, it is cozier than prayer time. It is a place and a special time where I invite Him to sit next to me and I share or read my gratitude to Him.

There is no way that we could share all, but we can try. It is okay if I start to cry because He is patient and He is not in a hurry to leave. The secret place is that extra time that we spend with the Lord and therefore is according to each Christian and whenever they feel led to do so. In my secret place, I can then thank Him for my friends and what each one means to me. Although I pray for them often, I love to share with Him what a joy they are and just how 'perfectly' He matched them to me.

"The thief cometh not, but to steal, and to kill, and to destroy: I am come that they might have life, and that they might have it more abundantly." **John 10:10**

The secret place can be a place of abundance for us. It is that extra blessing of having Him alone to share our very heart, as if He doesn't already know. Finally, the secret place is not to be our prayer closet. This is that special place that you have set aside for Him. It is a quiet, relaxed, most comfortable seat that you desire to sit when you are relaxing.

Go find that place if you do not already have it. Invite Jesus over. Make a list, share your heart and let Him know just how much you love and appreciate Him.

QUESTIONS TO PONDER

Do you have a secret place where you spend time with the Lord?

Are there times that you tell Him how much you love and appreciate all that He has done in your life?

What is one of your favorite verses in the bible or your favorite passage?

What is the difference between a 'secret place' and a 'prayer closet'?

How often do you visit your special place?

Relationships

SISTERS

Sisters in Christ

"We have a little sister and she hath no breast; what shall we do for our sister in the day when she shall be spoken for?" **Song of Solomon 8:8**

GOSSIP, HATRED, JEALOUSY, envy, strife, backbiting, front biting, and every other ungodly thing has been around since Norah's Ark. Could you imagine if there had to be two women of each race on the ark? I am sure that it would have never reached dry land! Thank God that He did not choose to do things that way. He had a better plan for Noah and his family. As sisters in Christ we have to go back and adapt some of the old time ways.

When I was younger, women stood close together. They nurtured one another's children and they disciplined them if they needed it. Women cared and complimented each other. They cleaned houses for another working mother. They shared recipes, baked and prayed with and for each other. They sent letters, cards, ironed clothes, made family meals, went shopping together, saved seats for each other at church or other special events that they attended and they were involved in each other's families. I am not saying that women do not do these things today – many do and even far exceed the things mentioned above. However, overall some of the closeness and the strong love has diminished a bit.

The word of God has much to say about the importance of friends. Jesus was close friends with Mary and Martha and their brother Lazarus. He had a deep, deep love for them. The shortest scripture in the bible was when Lazarus died. It displays human compassion. *Jesus wept.* **John 11:35**

So Jesus always leaves a perfect example for us to follow, and in this case it's the importance of having a friend - a close friend that we can love, pray with/for and embrace. Some ladies have what I am speaking of but not every lady does so we need to reach out more to reach more about the power of a faithful Christian friend.

I am well aware that we live in the 21st century and that things are not done the same. We do now live in a 'super microwave society' and everything is done 'quickly' and in a 'hurry' and in a 'go-get-it-yourself' type of way. Women today have a completely different attitude, view and response to life issues. Some have been forced to take on the role of mother and father in their homes and from my perspective – on average they do it well and are to be commended. Getting involved in a local church or attending a good women's conference is not always affordable nor is time readily available. Sometimes we all need to pause and make time, for we are our neighbor's keeper according to the word of God.

Where is the Christian woman within us, which God has called us to be? *In the shadow of the steeples* women are hurting, lonely and dying spiritually. Go back and read the verse from the Solomon scripture. Solomon asked a good question – How shall we help our sister? Everyone that God created has a flaw. He did that on purpose. Why? So that no one would think that they were perfect, although some do, but according to Him they are not. God gave us all, both a spiritual and an emotional need which is that we all need someone to make it through life.

"Two are better than one; because they have a good reward for their labour." **Ecclesiastes 4:9**

So how can we help our sister? **Ecclesiastes Verse 10** reads, *"I am a wall, and my breast like towers; then was I in his eyes as one that found favour."*

Every woman can find themselves in the Song of Solomon – He has mentioned the breast, the thighs, the lips, the eyes, the arms, the cheeks, the heart, the neck, and the teeth. The complexion and even the kiss are all included in this chapter. God did not give us all the same size body and shape, but to not embrace what He has created in us would almost be saying that He made a mistake and we know that He has never made a mistake. We are to embrace what He has created. We are to compliment ad uplift other women and encourage them as we would want to be encouraged.

We can all recommit to pointing others to Jesus for salvation and the love that He provides. As Christian sisters, dare to never doubt the power of His everlasting love and magnificent calling on our lives. Reach in, reach out, and always reach up to Him for strength to make it from day to day.

"I will not fail thee, nor forsake thee." **Joshua 1:5**

The Lord is our strength and He will always be there to provide what we need in us. We cannot always count on man but He will never fail us. We will not have to look far. There are sisters that need our prayers, attention and loving embrace. There are even some that need a good spiritual mentor. Solomon's question is only the beginning of many other questions that we all encounter. Together we can reach in, reach out, and most definitely continue to reach up to the only 'One' that has all of the answers – The Lord Jesus Christ.

QUESTIONS TO PONDER

Do you have a friend like the one described in this devotional?

_____

_____

Are you a friend like the one described in this devotional towards someone else?

_____

_____

What is the importance of such a friend?

_____

_____

What are some things that you can improve upon in regards to being a friend?

_____

_____

What kinds of things can you do as a friend to assist your sister in 'need'?

_____

_____

COMPANIONS

At The Same Hour

FROM GALILEE, the same city where Jesus performed His first miracle: there came a man whose son was sick. **John 4: 47-54** reads *"**47**When he heard that Jesus was come out of Judaea into Galilee, he went unto him, and   besought him that he would come down and heal his son: for he was at the point of death. **48**Then said Jesus unto him, except you see signs and wonders, ye will not believe. **49**The nobleman saith unto him, Sir, come down here my child die. **50**Jesus saith unto him, Go thy way; thy son liveth. And the man believed the word that Jesus had spoken unto him, and he went his way. **51**And as he was now going down, his servants met him, and told him, saying, Thy son liveth. **52**Then enquired he of them to amend. And they said unto him, yesterday at the seventh hour the fever left him. **53**So the father knew that it was at the same hour in which Jesus said unto him, Thy son liveth: and himself believed, and his whole house. **54**This is again the second miracle that Jesus did, when he was come out of Judaea."*

There have been numerous 'at the same hour' times in our lives. Only heaven will reveal those times when the Lord Jesus answered many of our prayers in the hour of our particular need. During Jesus' time on earth, He went about performing miracles all around town from city to city. In His own home some miracles He could not perform, not because of Him, but because of a lack of faith of the people there.

In **John 4** we read of the second miracle of Jesus, it is quite interesting that as all other passages in the bible they are all applicable to us. I can think of several times in my life that I may have mailed a card to a friend to remind them of His love for them and that I was praying for them. It may have been a simple thinking of you card, I would go to the mailbox and receive a card from them the day that they received mine. At the same time we were thinking of each other and our cards passed in the mail!

We all can relate to a phone call to or from someone and they or we would say, "I was just thinking of you as well." As exciting as these times are in our lives, it does not compare to the Lord answering our prayers at the same hour in which we are praying for a certain need. Would it not be awesome that when we get to heaven that the Lord would share with us all of the times that we were praying and He answered us at the same hour that we were praying? Can you imagine the times that we have prayed with or for family members and friends or the friends of a friend? God is interested in all of our prayers and some things that we have prayed He has answered right away and we all know well, yet there has been other times that we have had to wait a while for an answer, but we know that He always give a yes, no, or wait answer. The Lord Jesus never leaves us just waiting to hear back from Him when we pray.

Although we may not always witness the hour in which He answers a certain prayer, it is the excitement of knowing that, just as the nobleman we can believe and trust that He does all things according to His perfect will for us. Prayer and faith goes hand in hand, a part of believing is trusting as well. Being healed or praying for healing for someone else is not always God's plan for restored health, but because we do not know that ahead of time we are praying and trusting in Him because He knows what's best.

It is wise that in all of our prayers that we asking for His will to be done and not ours. Preparing our hearts for the unknown can be a very hard thing to do especially when we desire for it to turn out a certain way. Healing through the hands of the Lord is still prevalent today, be encouraged, always *pray without ceasing.* **1Thessalonians 5:17**. Never lose faith in God, even if your answer does not come at that hour be assured that an answer will come from Him. Trust God, not just for healing, trust Him with your life totally, He created you and He knows us completely. Offer up praises and supplications to Him right now, *'at this very hour'* He is there and He is waiting to hear your needs.

Healing does not only come from Him, but also through Him, trust and wait pray for doctors , nurses, and all the medical staff, the Lord has used so many of them to perform miraculous healing.

QUESTIONS TO PONDER

What was your most recent answer to prayer?

_____

_____

Are there times when you have felt so burdened about something that you felt as though you did not know 'what' to pray?

_____

_____

Is there a person that you enjoy sharing your prayer request with? What is their name? Why do you enjoy sharing with them?

_____

_____

Is there a person that you have been praying for that needs physical or spiritual healing? Who are they and what are their needs?

_____

_____

How much time do you spend praying for the needs of others? Could it be more?

_____

_____

FRIENDS

What Type Of Friend Are You?

A FEW YEARS AGO WWJD was the buzz word all over America people applied it to so many things and displayed it in several different ways. There were wristbands and tee shirts and mugs and bumper stickers and you name it! They even went as far to having a television show named from it. Well the question is still there although it is no longer the buzz word for today. WWJD shall always be a question with a definite answer to it. In every circumstance God has let us His response to them in the bible.

In **Job 16:1-4** Job was going through a hard time and to be encouraged by his friends, however, they were not very helpful during his time of need. They made fun of him and told him that there must have been sin in his life to go through all that he was going through. Job's response to them was **verse 2** *"I have heard many such things: miserable comforters are ye all."* In **verse 4** he said, *"I could also speak as you do: if your soul was in my soul's stead, I could heap up words against you, and shake my head at you."*

Job's friends were not caring nor were they offering words of encouragement to him.

We know what Jesus would do because He allowed it to prove the loyalty of Job towards Him. What would you have done? What type of friend are you? I truly would like to think that I would have not reacted in the manner in which Job's friends did I also would think that it would all be contingent upon where I am spiritually. As Christians we do not always respond to situations in a biblical way. Sometimes we feel bad when we realize that we mishandle a situation, then should go back and make a mends for it. I could only imagine how Job felt at this time when he was in need of a friend to console him.

There was more than one of them and surely there should have been one to influence the others of a more positive way to be a blessing to Job. He had already encountered a negative response from his wife. **Verse 2:9** explains, *"Then said his wife unto him, Dost thou still retain thine integrity? Curse God and die."* Thank the Lord that Job's latter was greater than his beginning. **Verse 42:12** *"So the Lord blessed the latter end of Job more than his beginning:"*

Job, just as many of us, did not receive the encouragement that he needed during his time of trial, especially from those that were the closest to him. Every word in the bible is written so that when we find ourselves in those predicaments we will know the correct to respond spiritually. The Lord equipped us with a wealth of wisdom from Himself, He loves us and He wants us to succeed as close as we can in the flesh in our Christian journey. We too can always draw strength from His word no matter what life sends our way.

The final thought and question is what type of friend are you?

Job 19:14 reads, *"My kinsfolk have failed, and my familiar friends have forgotten me."*

Job 16:20 reads, *"My friends scorn me: but mine eye poureth out tears unto God."*

Job felt lonely at this time yet he continued to cry out to the Lord. It is clear that he needed friends at least one that would have encouraged him. This is still a lesson for us to learn from, because they may be times when we experience what he did and we would have to cry out to the Lord. Here are just a few friend scriptures found in the bible that describes a friend.

Proverbs 27:6 *reads, "Faithful are the wounds of a friend; but the kisses of an enemy are deceitful."*

Proverbs 17:17 reads, *"A friend loveth at all times, and a brother is born for adversity."*

Proverbs 27:17 reads, *"Iron sharpenth iron, so a man the countenance of his friend."*

Proverbs 18:24 reads, *"A man that hath friends must shew himself friendly: and there is a friend that sticketh closer than a brother."*

There are other verses that we can relate to about the role of a Christian friend. One thing we must all remember about friends and being a friend is also found in the bible in.

In Job's case he did not receive what he may have given to his friends, just as we might not always receive from our friends what we expect from them when we are in need of being encouraged. Nevertheless that does not exempt us from being a faithful friend. When the time comes, I only pray that we would be a Job and say as he said in **Job 13:15** *"Though he slay me, yet will I trust in him, but I will maintain mine own ways before him."* Just as the Lord allowed Job to go through the things that he did, we will at some point encounter the same.

We just need to be ready as a friend to do as Jesus would do and be the friend that He has called us to be. *"…and there is a friend that sticketh closer than a brother."* **Proverbs 18:24**. And that Friend is **JESUS**!

QUESTIONS TO PONDER

Do you have a real friend? What makes them real?

_____

_____

Are you a real friend? How do you know?

_____

_____

Is it hard to be a real friend?

_____

_____

Can anyone be as good of a friend as Jesus? Why or why not?

_____

_____

What can you do to be an even better friend?

_____

_____

Our Father

STRENGTH

Satan's Desire

LATELY, I have been committing myself to *enhancing* my time reading the Bible. I could never devote enough time meditating on God's word. Humanly it can be a challenge to work a job and come home to a long list of things that need to be done. Our strength comes from The Lord, He is the very air that we breathe. As I am sitting and thinking, **Luke 22:31** comes to my mind, *"And the Lord said Simon, Simon behold Satan hath desired to have you, that he may sift you as wheat:"* We could easily replace our name for Simons. It is most definitely Satan's desire to do the same to us. Satan wants nothing more than to *pull us apart spiritually* and to cause us to doubt. He has many things that he desires to do with us.

It would give Satan gladness to see us not display joy in our lives and to second guess our salvation. He delights when he recognizes that we often faint in well doing. *"And let us not be weary in well doing: for in due season we will shall reap, if we faint not."* **Galatians 6:9**

By nature we all struggle from time to time, but when it becomes the norm for us we need to be encouraged through God's word. None of us walk, on a regular basis, as strongly as we should. We all need a good Christian friend in our life that will be in tuned with us and know just when we need to be encouraged.

The Lord knew that we would struggle that is why He gave us **Luke 22:32** that reads, *"But I have prayed for thee, that thou faith fail not: and when thou are converted, strengthen thy brethren."* Jesus knows what we are, where we are, and that is why He has placed family and friends in our lives to help us remain encouraged. When we do not have those people there as Christians we are to then remember to encourage ourselves in Him.

There are times in our lives that we need to hold on tighter to His word and to claim His godly principles for us. We should determine that it's His strength that we must go in and not our own. It is His strength that will sustain us and we dare not try to endure in our fleshly strength. We must remember that when the tide is the highest, that's when the current is the strongest. We should never try to 'Walk on Water' unless Jesus bids us to come!!!

He is the Master of the storm and the sea in our lives. He is our 'Lifesaver', through Him we shall never perish! Yes, Satan desires to sift all Christians as wheat, but the Lord is in control of all. What a comfort it is to know that no matter where we are in life, no matter what state we are in, Jesus is truly a shelter in a time of storm. Satan can desire all that he wants and yet we can rest assured that he has little power, because God has 'All Power'.

As Christian we need to remember and remind others of the security that we possess through Christ and that there are no problems that are too hard for God. Lastly we must also remember and remind other Christians that Satan only wants to 'sift' that which is SAVED!

QUESTIONS TO PONDER

Have you ever felt Satan's pull on your life? What happened?

_____

_____

Do you get tired spiritually? How is that different from being physically tired?

_____

_____

Do you have a 'Godfriend'? Who is your partner in Christ? How do they encourage you? How can we encourage ourselves?

_____

_____

What does this phrase mean to you: "When the tide is highest, that's when the current is strongest?"

_____

_____

Why is Satan only concerned with 'sifting' Christians?

_____

_____

TIMELY

I'm Going To Tell My Daddy!

"And because ye are sons, God hath sent forth the Spirit of his Son into your hearts, crying Abba, Father." **Galatians 4:6**

REMEMBER THAT EXPRESSION when we were younger? I sure do! I remember saying that when my siblings didn't give me what I thought I should have gotten from them. Well, as adults we can still use that 'catchy phrase'. We can tell our heavenly Father no matter what it is - He is concerned. **Psalms 34:19** reads, *"Call unto me, and I will answer thee and show thee great and mighty things, which thou knowest not."*

Every word in the bible is true and God truly wants us to call on him when we are in need of Him. So many times we try to fix things on our own instead of going to Him immediately.

We allow the devil to place pride in our hearts, thinking that no one cares and that we can master the problem on our own. He often gives us the feeling that if God loved us then He really would not have allowed this to happen to us. He renders to us excuse after excuse of reasons why we should not get others involved and he lies to us constantly because that's his job and he does his job very well!

He is the last one and the least one that wants us to tell Jesus anything. His purpose is to keep us as far away from the throne of God as he possibly can. The devil is a deceiver and when he has used all of his tricks, he then will entice us to follow our hearts and not God. **Jeremiah 17:9** tells us about our heart, *"For the heart is deceitful and above all things, and desperately wicked: who can know it?"*

As Christians we need to stay on our knees as when life's problems arise, better yet be there before problems come. There will be many issues in our Christian journey, and as the Lord tarries in His coming, we will often feel the need to say 'I'm going to tell Daddy.' It will not surprise Him, He is waiting to hear it from us, so we are really just telling Him again for He knows and sees all things.

We should all go to the Father with every concern. The battle is not ours, but the Lord's. **Jeremiah 32:27** reads, *"Behold, I am the Lord, the God of all flesh: is there anything too hard for me?"* What a joy to know that we can call on Him and not only get an answer, but be assured that nothing is too hard for Him! We can be the one to stand in the gap for our family.

I beseech you to fight all battles on our knees and not always face to face. **Philippians 4:6-7** reads, *"Be careful for nothing; but in everything by prayer and supplications with thanksgiving let your request be made known unto God. And the peace of God, which passeth all understanding, shall keep your hearts and minds through Christ Jesus."*

So go ahead tell the Father, for He is waiting to hear and to answer your call.

QUESTIONS TO PONDER

How do you feel knowing that the Lord is always there to hear our prayers and needs?

_____

_____

How much time do you spend praying for yourself and the needs of others?

_____

_____

Are there times that you are very anxious to share a need with the Lord?

_____

_____

What do you do while you wait for God to answer your prayer?

_____

_____

Do you remember to pray first or do you try to fix things yourself? Elaborate.

_____

_____

INTIMACY

How Do You View Jesus?

"But we see Jesus, who was made a little lower than the angels for the suffering of death, crowned with glory and honour: that he by the grace of God should taste death for every man." **Hebrews 2:9**

JESUS HAS many names all throughout the bible. He is *'The Great Physician'*, *'The Healer'*, *'The Deliverer'*, *'The Great I Am'*, *'The Star of David'*, *'The Alpha and Omega'*.

There are many names for Him listed in the bibles as well as there are names that we use to describe Him. How do we view Jesus? This is the question that I am posing in this devotion.

After we realize, that God gave His only begotten Son that we may have eternal life, if we believe on Him. **John 3:16** Once we have accepted His free gift, how do we view Him? I am not asking what He has done in our lives or the lives of our loved ones. I am asking how we view Him after we are saved. When we are in need of guidance, comfort or a sense of belonging, how does He fit into these needs?

Do we ever think that He is concerned about these needs? There should be a time in our lives that we realize that without Him we can do nothing. **John 30:16**

We need Him at all times, in all ways and all aspects of our lives. If we are to succeed in or at anything He must be in the midst of it. We can not only call on Him when things are not working as we'd planned. Jesus must be fully involved from the beginning until the very end of all that we endeavor to do.

He said in **Jeremiah 33: 3** *"Call unto me, and I will answer thee, and show thee great and mighty things, which thou knowest not."* When we learn to place Him first in all things, then we can began to accept His will when things do not turn out as we have planned.

Having the correct view of who Jesus is, is simply realizing that He must be in the midst of "All'. Does this mean that we will always understand when our circumstances do not come together as we expect them? No, God tells us what His ways are in **Isaiah 55:8-9** which reads, *"For my thoughts are not your thoughts, neither are your ways my ways, saith the Lord. For as the heavens are higher than the earth, so are my ways higher than yours, and my thoughts your thoughts."*

God knows what is best for us, and He only allows what He deems is the perfect will for our lives. He was the God/Man who dwelt among the earth so that He would experience life as a human being, yet He was without sin. **Nahum 1:2(a)** tells us that He is a jealous God. When we fail to include Him in every part of our lives, He is jealous. Why? He created us to enjoy fellowship with Him. That is why He told us to call upon Him in **Isaiah 55:8**. God is always waiting and available for us!

If we were asked to compile a list with our needs listed on one side and a reliable person's name across from that need an example would be if I wrote lonely and troubled on my list across from them I would naturally place my spouse's name, without thinking that it should be Jesus/ spouse. We often do not remember that Jesus is totally concerned about every need that we have. The more time that we spend reading our bibles our view of how we view Him would become so much clearer.

We should challenge ourselves, if we are not already doing so to find a relative or friend to join our spiritual walk with the Lord. We all need a spiritual companion that would share with us in prayer and praises to The Lord. We all need to take out our 'spiritual lens' and gain a closer view of Jesus. We need to include Him more in the areas that we have forgotten to. Every Christian should desire a better vision of Him. How do you view Jesus?

QUESTIONS TO PONDER

What names do you use to describe Jesus?

_____

_____

Are there times when you have forgotten to
include him?

_____

_____

Did you realize it right away? What was taking
place in your life?

_____

_____

Would you say that there are areas in your life
that you need a clearer vision of Jesus? If so,
what areas?

_____

_____

Who is God to you?

_____

_____

The Final Chapter

THE END

"And as it is appointed unto men once to dies, but after this the judgment." **Hebrews 9:27**

JUST AS ALL books have a final chapter or an end, so does our life. Unless the Lord returns to take His children home we will all face death. Where will you spend eternity? It would seem foolish to me to write this devotional about God and not properly try and introduce Him to those that may not know Him.

I'm not going to give an easy quick formula that says do this and you are saved, but I will say that if you simply believe in what God's Son Jesus did on the cross as your only way to heaven you can be saved.

For those that would say, "I never realized that I needed a savior" or "I want to know more about Jesus and trust Him for eternal life" please continue to read.

If you are sure that you at some time in your life accept His free give God bless you, continue to share the gospel.

For my friends that are lost please perform the following:

1. Admit that you are in need of his saving power and cannot get to Heaven on your own.

Romans 3:23 reads, *"For all have sinned, and come short of the glory of God."*

2. Believe on the Lord Jesus Christ and His finished work on the Cross.

Romans 10:9 reads, *"That if thou shalt confess with thy mouth the Lord Jesus, and shalt believe in thine heart that God hath raised him from the dead, thou shalt be saved."*

3. Confess that you are a sinner and believe in your heart that only He can save you.

Romans 10:10 reads, *"For with the heart man believeth unto righteousness; and with the mouth confession is made unto salvation."*

4. Pray your prayer of repentance

I John 5:13 reads, *"Those things have I written unto you that believe on the name of the son of God; that ye may know that ye have eternal life, and that ye, may believe on the name of the son of God."*

When you pray, you share with him your very heart. The God of the bible shall never leave your heart or soul. You cannot lose your salvation ever if you have truly believed on Him.

May God bless and keep you!

Journal

THE FOLLOWING PAGES are provided so that you may track your growth as a Christian.

Six months from now, use the space provided to write down your progress. Then in a year, review your initial place, your six month growth and compare it to where you are after a year of meditation on God's word.

God bless you,

Attitude

Six Months: Date _____

Where are you?

_____

_____

_____

_____

One Year: Date _____

What has changed?

_____

_____

_____

_____

Faith

Six Months: Date _____

Where are you?

_____

_____

_____

_____

_____

One Year: Date _____

What has changed?

_____

_____

_____

_____

_____

Manipulation

Six Months: Date _____

Where are you?

_____

_____

_____

_____

One Year: Date _____

What has changed?

_____

_____

_____

_____

Love

Six Months: Date _____

Where are you?

_____

_____

_____

_____

One Year: Date _____

What has changed?

_____

_____

_____

_____

Pain

Six Months: Date _____

Where are you?

_____

_____

_____

_____

_____

One Year: Date _____

What has changed?

_____

_____

_____

_____

_____

Change

Six Months: Date _____

Where are you?

_____

_____

_____

_____

_____

One Year: Date _____

What has changed?

_____

_____

_____

_____

_____

Prayer

Six Months: Date _____

Where are you?

_____

_____

_____

_____

_____

One Year: Date _____

What has changed?

_____

_____

_____

_____

_____

Endurance

Six Months: Date _____

Where are you?

_____

_____

_____

_____

One Year: Date _____

What has changed?

_____

_____

_____

_____

Meditation

Six Months: Date _____

Where are you?

_____

_____

_____

_____

_____

One Year: Date _____

What has changed?

_____

_____

_____

_____

_____

Sisters

Six Months: Date _____

Where are you?

_____

_____

_____

_____

_____

One Year: Date _____

What has changed?

_____

_____

_____

_____

_____

Companionship

Six Months: Date _____

Where are you?

_____

_____

_____

_____

_____

One Year: Date _____

What has changed?

_____

_____

_____

_____

Friends

Six Months: Date _____

Where are you?

_____

_____

_____

_____

_____

One Year: Date _____

What has changed?

_____

_____

_____

_____

_____

Strength

Six Months: Date _____

Where are you?

_____

_____

_____

_____

One Year: Date _____

What has changed?

_____

_____

_____

_____

Timely

Six Months: Date _____

Where are you?

_____

_____

_____

_____

_____

One Year: Date _____

What has changed?

_____

_____

_____

_____

Intimacy

Six Months: Date _____

Where are you?

_____

_____

_____

_____

_____

One Year: Date _____

What has changed?

_____

_____

_____

_____

_____

the **Butterfly Typeface**

"Making good GREAT"

WWW.THEBUTTERFLYTYPEFACE.COM

www.ingramcontent.com/pod-product-compliance
Lightning Source LLC
Chambersburg PA
CBHW052109090426
42741CB00009B/1742